Tilda's SUMMER IDEAS

A DAVID & CHARLES BOOK

Copyright © Tone Finnanger 2010
Originally published as *Tildas Sommarideer*

First published in the UK in 2010 by David & Charles
Reprinted in 2011
David & Charles is an F+W Media Inc. company
4700 East Galbraith Road
Cincinnati, OH 45236

A catalogue record for this book is available from the
British Library.

ISBN-13: 978-0-7153-3864-3 paperback
ISBN-10: 0-7153-3864-1 paperback

Printed in China by Toppan Leefung
for David & Charles
Brunel House, Newton Abbot, Devon

Stylist Ingrid Skaansar
Photography Ragnar Hartvig

David & Charles publish high quality books on a
wide range of subjects.
For more great book ideas visit: **www.rucraft.co.uk**

Colourful Summer

Spring and summer are just around the corner and now's the time to start creating lighter and brighter surroundings. At this time of year it feels natural to create with playful colours, capturing the essence of spring and summer.

In this book you will find ideas for Kitchen and Garden angels, a variety of colourful garlands, traditional Swedish Dala horses and some lovely papercraft ideas to help bring some sun and summer into your home!

The projects are made using the latest Tilda collections Kitchengarden and Flowergarden, using shades of turquoise, green, pink and red. It has been a great pleasure designing this spring's new Tilda range and I hope you'll find some projects here you'd like to make. But remember, the real value is in the pattern, so feel free to use materials you already have, or combine old and new.

This is the second booklet in the Tilda range, with the aim of giving you some ideas to use with the season's new products. You will find more ideas and projects in the full Tilda books.

Wishing you a wonderful and creative spring and summer!

Enjoy!

Tone Finnanger

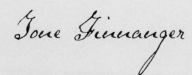

Contents

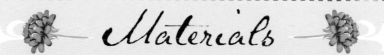

Materials

We have used Tilda fabrics, buttons and ribbons to make the figures in this booklet. Tilda products are designed by Tone Finnanger and are produced and distributed by Panduro Hobby.

Tilda products can be purchased at **www.pandurohobby.co.uk**

Read more about Tilda at **www.tildasworld.com**

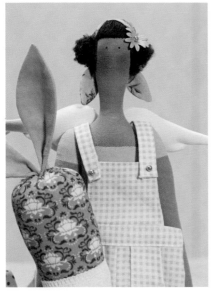

HAIR

Make the fringe using the same embroidery yarn as the hair. Embroidery yarn in suitable hair colours is available from the Tilda range. Draw a line using a vanishing marker or a thin pen with pale ink over the forehead, so you have a guide for sewing the fringe. Sew a fringe with small stitches using the embroidery yarn, then sew some longer stitches down over the cheek on each side, see figure A.

FACES

We recommend you add the hair before marking the eyes to ensure they are correctly positioned. Stick two pins into the head to check where the eyes should sit. Remove the pins. Use the eye tool from the Tilda Face Painting set (ref. no. 713400) or make the eyes (where the pin holes are) by dipping a pin head in some black paint and pressing onto the face. Make rosy cheeks by applying some lipstick or blusher with a dry brush, after the eyes have dried.

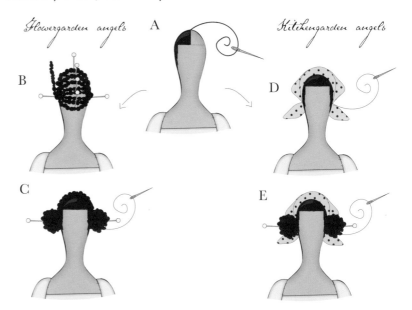

Flowergarden angels   A   *Kitchengarden angels*

B   D

C   E

Flowergarden angels

Stick pins into the forehead and over the centre to the back of the head. Also insert a pin in each side of the head. Wind the hair back and forth between the pins on each side of the head and between the pins in the middle, see figure B. When the head is covered, stitch the hair in place and remove the pins. Then sew a bunch of hair onto each side of the head, see figure C.

Kitchengarden angels

Sew the scarf as described in the instructions. Pin the middle of the scarf to the centre of the head, so the fringe is visible. Fold the middle of the scarf over the back of the head and tie a knot with the sides to hold it in place. Fasten with a few stitches and remove the pin, see figure D. Make a little bunch of hair for each side of the head and sew in place, see figure E.

SEWING

Avoid cutting out the figure beforehand unless absolutely necessary. Fold the fabric double, right sides facing, and transfer the pattern onto it. Mark the openings for reversing.

CUTTING OUT

Cut out the figure with a narrow seam allowance, 3–4mm (1/8 in) is ideal. Extra seam allowance is required at the reversing sections, approx 7–8mm (3/8 in). Cut notches in the seam allowance where the seam curves sharply.

REVERSING

Use a florist's stick to help with reversing. As a rule, use the blunt end, though the pointed end can be used carefully for small details. To avoid piercing the fabric, just cut off the top millimetre of the tip.

Long, thin pieces such as legs can be reversed by pressing the blunt end against the foot, see figure A. Starting at the foot, pull the leg over the stick, see figure B. Continue to pull the leg over the stick until the foot appears at the top. Holding the foot, pull the rest of the leg over until it is completely turned right side out, see figure C. Turn the arms in the same way.

STUFFING

Fold in the extra seam allowance by the openings in the seam, with the exception of the legs for the angels, where the seam allowance is tucked into the body and should not therefore be folded in. Iron the figure.

When stuffing, use your finger to push the wadding in as far as you can, and use a pen or similar to push into the parts you cannot reach. If the implement is too thin it will just push through the filling.

Push the wadding loosely into the figure and try to avoid over-stuffing, which will cause lumps to form. Add wadding to each section until correctly stuffed and continue to add wadding until you have a perfectly formed figure.

Sew up the openings.

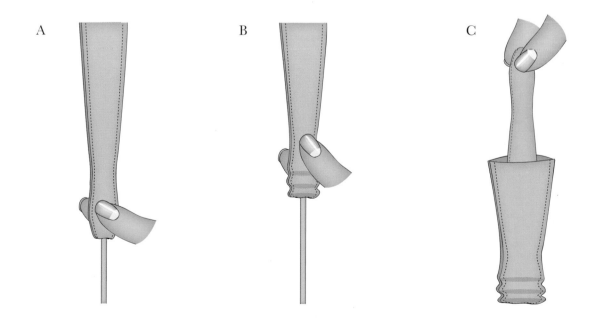

A   B   C

Kitchengarden angels, green cushions and a birdhouse create a cosy summer setting. The birdhouse is part of the Tilda range and can be used as a decoration indoors and a real birdhouse outdoors. We recommend you trim the perch or push it in further to discourage predators.

Seed Sachets

Copy the seed sachet pattern on pages 45–46 onto paper or card.

Cut out the sachets and apply glue to the edges. Fold in the glued edges and fold the sachet double to glue it together. Make a hole with a hole punch in the top of the sachet.

We recommend that you fold the seeds in paper before placing them in the sachet.

Patterns can be found on pages 34–38

YOU WILL NEED

Various fabrics for the skin, clothes and wings
Tilda hair
Embroidery yarn for the fringe
Craft rubber for sandals
3mm (⅛ in) beads or similar
Tilda paper flowers
Lace (optional)

HOW TO MAKE

BODY
Sew together the skin fabric and the light turquoise fabric so the join is approximately where shown in the pattern. Fold the joined fabrics double, right sides facing.

Do the same with the skin fabric and the fabric for the arms and legs. Transfer all patterns, see figure A.

Cut out all parts and cut notches in the seam allowance where it curves sharply.

Reverse the body, arms and legs as described on page 5.

Iron all sections. The seam allowance on the body and arms should be ironed in. Fill the lower part of the leg with wadding, until where indicated by the dashed line in the pattern. Sew a stitch across the knee before filling the rest of the leg, see figure B. Fill the body and arms. Insert the legs into the body and sew in place. Sew the arms to the body, see figure C.

DUNGAREES
Fold fabric for two pockets, upper section and waistband double. Transfer the patterns and sew around, see figure D.

Cut out and reverse. Iron all the parts. Sew a stitch along the curved top edge of the pockets and around the edge of the upper section, see figure E.

Cut out four trouser sections from the patterned green fabric and four lining sections from the dotted pink fabric.

Remember that two of the trouser sections and two of the lining sections should be reversed.

Sew the lining sections into the trouser legs so the join between the trouser and lining is approximately as shown in the pattern.

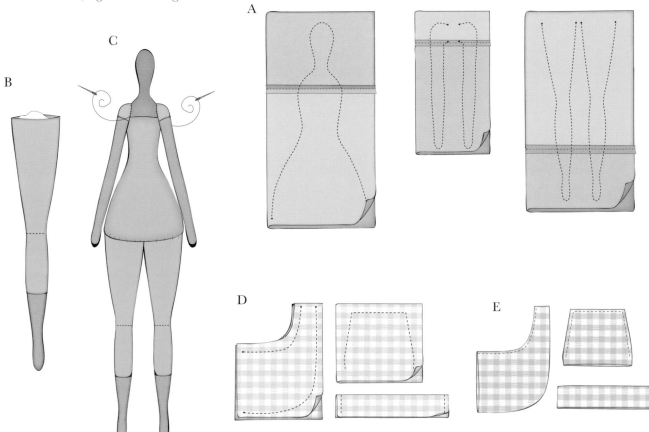

Place the trouser sections together two by two, right sides facing and sew the curved section, see figure F.

Fold out the parts. Sew on the pockets along the lower curved part of the pocket, at the front of the trousers. Sew a zig-zag stitch along the sides, see figure G.

Line up the seam allowance for the waistband and seam allowance for the upper section with the seam allowance for the front of the dungarees. The waistband should be in the middle. Sew a stitch approximately where the seam allowance ends to attach the three parts, see figure H. Fold up the upper section and fold down and iron the seam allowance at the back of the trouser section. The waistband should then be folded down over the front of the trousers and cover the top part of the pockets. Sew along the edge to fix the top part of the pockets in place, see figure I.

Place the front of the trousers with the pockets, upper section and waistband, right sides facing, with the trouser backs and sew around, see figure J.

Trim allowances and iron the trousers. Iron in any allowance which is not sewn. Sew around the waist.

Iron in the lining at the bottom of each leg, see figure K. Turn up the bottom, see figure L and fasten with a few stitches inside the trousers.

Cut two strips of patterned green fabric 17 x 3cm (6½ x 1¼ in), adding seam allowance. Iron in the allowance along each length and also at one end, then iron each strip double. Sew around the edge of each strip to close the open side.

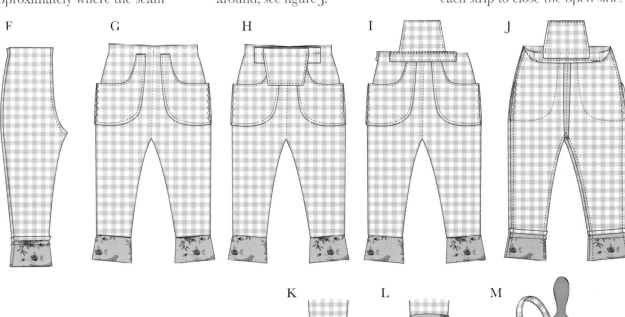

F G H I J

K L M

Put the dungarees on the figure, folding pleats around the waist. Use pins to hold the pleats and then sew the pleats, without sewing to the figure. Remove the pins.

Pin the shoulder straps at the back of the angel and the inside of the trousers. Cross them over at the back. Ensure the trousers are hanging at the correct length before fastening the straps with a bead at the upper section and then sewing at the back, see figure M.

SCARF
Fold the fabric for the scarf with right sides facing, transfer the pattern and sew round, see figure N on page 10. Cut out, reverse and iron.

Add the hair, fasten the scarf and create the face as described on page 2. Make the sandals as described on page 20.

11

WINGS

Fold the fabric for the wings double and transfer the pattern. Sew around the wings, see figure O.

Reverse and iron. Sew the seams as shown in the pattern, see figure P. Fill the wings with wadding using the wooden stick and close the opening. Sew the wings onto the figure.

CLOTH

Fold the fabric for the cloth with right sides facing and sew three sides.

Cut out and reverse. Iron the cloth. Sew a piece of lace along the bottom edge, see figure Q. Sew the top of the cloth inside the pocket.

Sew a small flower into the angel's hair with a small bead. Sew a piece of lace around each leg. Put the hands inside the pockets, see figure R.

N
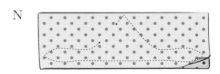

O

P

Q

R

12

Radishes

Patterns can be found on page 40

YOU WILL NEED

Fabric for radishes
Fabric for leaves
Lace, if using

HOW TO MAKE

Sew together a strip of pink/red fabric and a strip of white fabric so the border between the two is approximately where shown in the pattern.

Fold the sewn section double, right sides facing and transfer the radish pattern.

Sew around, see figure A. Fold fabric for leaves double, right sides facing, transfer patterns for two leaves and sew around.

Cut out, reverse and iron the radish and leaves. Iron in the seam allowance at the radish's opening.

Sew around the opening with embroidery yarn. Stuff the radish and insert the leaves before sewing up the opening, see figure B.

Sew a few stitches to fasten the leaves and pull the yarn tight.

If using, sew some lace around the radish.

A

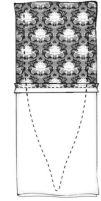

B

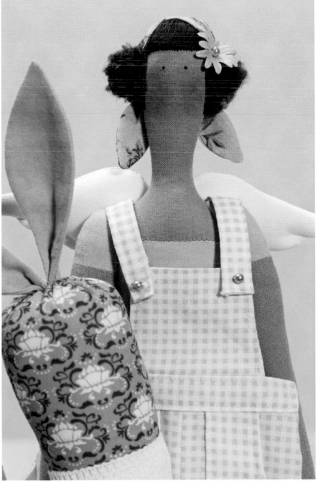

13

Summer Garlands

*Patterns can be found on
page 41*

YOU WILL NEED

Skin fabric
Tilda hair
Embroidery yarn for hair
Fabric for dresses
Flower buttons
Radishes, see page 13
Ribbon for hanging

INSTRUCTIONS

BODY
Fold the skin fabric double, transfer the pattern and sew round the body and arms, see figure A.

You will need a minimum of two figures to make the garland. Cut out, fold inside out and iron the parts. Iron in the seam allowance at the opening on the arms.

Fill the body and arms and sew up the opening in the body. Sew the arms onto each side of the figure, see figure B.

A
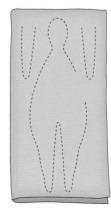

B
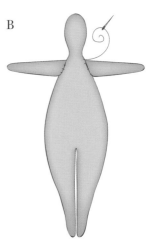

DRESS

Cut two pieces of fabric for the dress 15.5 x 17cm (6¼ x 6½ in), adding plenty of seam allowance at each end. Measure approx 6cm (2½ in) below one end at each side of each dress section and fold in the corners so the edge folds over the top. Iron the top edge, insert a piece of embroidery yarn approx 40cm (16 in) in length, and sew up, see figure C.

Do the same with the other dress fabric and insert the same length of yarn. Position the dress with right sides facing and sew up the side. Iron and sew up the seam allowance at the base of the dress, see figure D. Reverse the dress, put onto the figure and tie the ends of the embroidery yarn at one end so the dress is pulled tight around the neck, see figure E.

Make three radishes from page 13, or three hearts between the figures. Make the hearts by folding the fabric, right sides facing, transferring the pattern and sewing around. Cut out, reverse, iron and fill. Sew up the opening, then sew the figures together and tie a ribbon at each end to hang from.

C

D

E

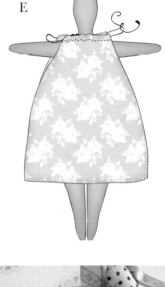

Make this beautiful summer setting in your kitchen in the shades of turquoise, red and pink. The Flowergarden angel can be found on page 22.

Flag Garlands

Patterns can be found on page 39

Using embroidered flower appliqués from the Tilda range and pom-pom ribbon, we've given this flag garland a modern twist. Fold the fabric for the flag, right sides facing, then transfer the flag pattern and sew up the sides. Cut out, reverse and iron. Sew a zig-zag stitch along the open end to hold it together.

Cut a strip of fabric as long as you want the garland to be, and 4.5cm (1¾ in) wide. Iron in approx 7mm (3/8 in) on each side of the strip and iron it double to make it approx 1.5cm (5/8 in) wide. Insert the flag edges with zig-zag stitching in between the two layers of the strip and pin in place. Sew along the open side of the strip to fasten the flags in place. Sew the pom-pom ribbon along the bottom edge of the strip and sew the flower appliqué onto some of the flags.

Lanterns

We recommend you use a glass which is relatively straight. Measure the circumference around the top and bottom of the glass, plus its height, and transfer the measurements onto card. Cut out and check that the pattern fits the glass. Transfer the pattern onto fabric and add seam allowance when cutting out.

Iron in the seam allowance at the top and bottom with Vlisofix or stitch to fasten. Fold the fabric, right sides facing, and sew up the open side. Pull the fabric over the glass from the narrowest end up and decorate by sewing or gluing on ribbon, beads and appliqué.

Bags

Patterns can be found on page 43

YOU WILL NEED

Fabric for bag, handle and lining
Extra stiff bag Vlisofix
Fabric and ribbon for decoration (optional)

HOW TO MAKE

The striped decoration on the bag is done in the same way as on the hearts, see page 26. Decorate the front bag section before sewing the bag together. The bag and lining pattern is marked double fold and should be double. The bag pattern is wider than the lining pattern, as the bag fabric will be hemmed along the edge.

Cut out two bag sections and two lining sections in your chosen fabrics. Cut out two pieces of stiff Vlisofix measuring 19.5 x 7.5cm (7¾ x 3 in) with seam allowance only along the ends, and cut out pieces of fabric measuring 19.5 x 15cm (7¾ x 6 in) with seam allowance all the way round. Place the glue side of the bag, Vlisofix against one half of the fabric and iron on. Iron the seam allowance along one edge around the Vlisofix, see figure A. Take one bag section with Vlisofix and the lining and sew up, see figure B.

Sew a large stitch along the top edge of the bag section to enable you to pull the string tight. Gather the fabric so that the bag is the same width as the lining and edge.

Place the edge where the fabric is ironed in over the gathered edge of the bag section. Fasten with pins and sew, see figure C.

Place the two bag sections with right sides facing and sew around, leaving the opening in the lining.

HANDLE

Cut a piece of bag Vlisofix 30 x 2cm (12 x ¾ in) without seam allowance, and a piece of fabric 30 x 4cm (12 x 1½ in), with plenty of seam allowance. Place the Vlisofix strip against one half of the fabric strip. Fold in the seam allowance along each side and fold the fabric strip double around the Vlisofix, see figure D. Sew a stitch along the open edge to fasten the layers.
Trim allowances, reverse and iron the bag. Push the lining down inside the bag.

Fasten the end of the handle onto each side inside the bag with pins. Sew a stitch around the top edge of the bag to fasten the handles and hold the lining in place, see figure D.

A

B

C

D

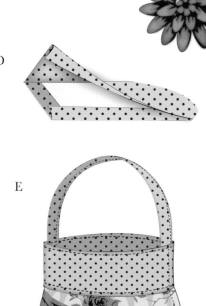

E

Flowergarden Angel

Patterns can be found on pages 34–35 and page 40

YOU WILL NEED

Different fabrics for the skin, clothes and wings
Tilda hair
Embroidery yarn for hair
Craft rubber for sandals
3mm (¹⁄₈ in) beads or similar
Tilda paper flowers

HOW TO MAKE

Sew the body and wings in the same way as for the Kitchengarden angel on page 8 and do the hair and face as described on page 4.

DRESS
Cut a piece of floral fabric 26 x 52cm (10½ x 20¾ in), adding plenty of seam allowance. Fold the fabric double to make it 26 x 26 cm (10½ x 10½ in) and sew the opposite open side, see figure A.

A

B

Reverse the dress and iron in the seam at the top and bottom. Sew up the seam allowance at the bottom.

Pin the dress around the midriff with small pleats. The dress should sit quite high up, see picture of the angel. Sew the dress around the body.

Fold the fabric for the belt double and transfer the pattern. Sew around the belt, remembering to leave a gap to turn it inside out, see figure B.

Cut out, reverse and iron the belt. Tie the belt around the angel's chest, with the knot to one side. Fasten with a few stitches so the ends sit nicely, see figure C.

Sew on the wings and sew on a paper flower and beads by the belt knot and in the hair, see figure D.

SANDALS
Copy the pattern for two sandals onto the craft rubber and cut out. Attach the craft rubber sandals with a few stitches under the foot. Attach a small flower with a bead in the middle of each sandal, see figure E.

C   D

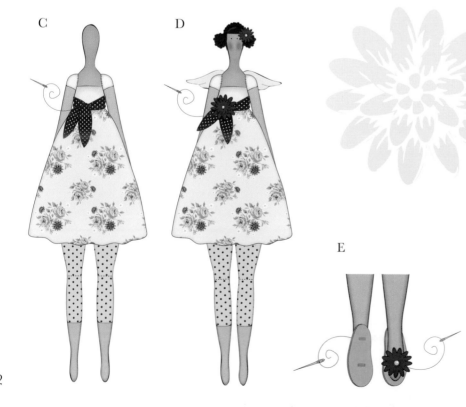

E

Dala Horses

Patterns can be found on page 44

YOU WILL NEED

Fabric for the body and mane
Vlisofix
Fabric or ribbon for decoration
Embroidery yarn
Beads for decoration

HOW TO MAKE

Embroidered details can be added before the horse is sewn together, but as the fabric stretches slightly, it is almost easier to do it at the end.

Cut two pieces of fabric large enough for the head and two pieces large enough for the body, using contrasting fabrics. Sew the head fabric and body fabric together so the border is approximately where shown in the pattern. Place the two body parts with right sides facing and sew around, see figure A.

Cut out, reverse, iron and fill the horse. Iron Vlisofix against the wrong side of a piece of fabric for the mane. Transfer the pattern from the pattern and cut out, without seam allowance. Iron the mane onto the horse.

Transfer the embroidery pattern as closely as possible with a vanishing marker or thin pen on the mane and head. Embroider with embroidery yarn in your chosen colour, as shown in the picture. Hide the knots at the seam between the head and body details where the ribbon will sit.

Cut strips of fabric 2cm (¾ in) wide plus seam allowance to use as ribbon. Iron in the seam allowance and sew the ribbon around the belly and neck of the horse. If you wish, sew a string of beads around the ribbon around the neck.

Trim the stick on a figure stand to the required length, sharpen the tip with a pencil sharpener and twist into the horse to enable it to stand stably.

YOU WILL NEED

Various complementary fabrics
Volume Vlisofix (optional)
Ribbon or flower appliqué (optional)

HOW TO MAKE

If you don't have inner cushions suitable for the shape you want to sew, iron a layer of volume Vlisofix against the wrong side of the cushion fabric for an even result. The cushion can then be filled with wadding. A quick solution for the impatient souls among us…

Square cushions do not need more detailed instructions, but in the picture you can see how you can use different fabrics together to make a range of matching cushions. Accompany with a few candle lanterns using the same fabric range and you'll soon have a brand new sitting room!

SIMPLE ROLL CUSHION

Cut out a centre fabric measuring approximately 44 x 44cm (17½ x 17½ in), and two side fabrics measuring 44 x 10cm (17½ x 4 in). Add seam allowance. Iron volume Vlisofix against the centre fabric to achieve a better shape. Sew the side fabrics to the centre fabric.

Fold in approx 5cm (2½ in) of the seam allowance on the outside of each end of the side pieces.

Iron in the seam allowance along the length and then fold a 2cm (¾ in) edge to make a tunnel for the cord. Sew the edge in place and thread the cord through, see figure A.

Sew on a ribbon, see figure B, before folding the cushion with right sides facing and sew up the open side. Reverse and iron the cushion. Draw the cords tight and tie. Decorate the cushion with a flower appliqué, if using.

A   B

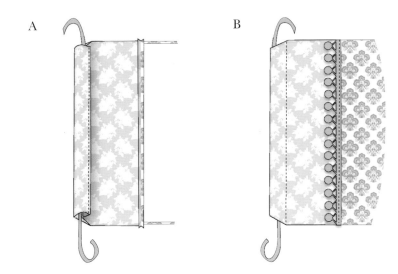

Hearts

Patterns can be found on page 42

YOU WILL NEED

Fabric for the hearts
Various fabrics and ribbons
for decoration
Ribbon for hanging

INSTRUCTIONS

Sewing strips of fabric and ribbon into shapes might not seem too exciting, but believe me, it's really great fun! Perhaps because you can get super results very quickly and you can play with so many different colours and patterns. Try using other patterns such as cushions or bags, as shown on page 21.

Cut two pieces of fabric large enough for the heart.

Find some suitable ribbons and cut strips of leftover fabric. Iron in the edges of the fabric strips, see figure A. Place the strip on the background and pin in place, see figure B. Sew along both sides of the ribbons and fabric strips to fasten. Iron the decorated fabric piece thoroughly and place it against the back piece, right sides facing.

Transfer the heart pattern and sew raound, see figure C.

Cut out, reverse and fill the heart. Sew up the opening and sew on a ribbon for hanging.

A

B

C

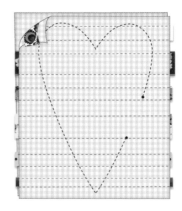

Notebooks

Cut approximately ten sheets of copier paper in half so that you have twenty sheets in A5 size.

Cut two pieces of decorative card in the same size. Place a pile of sheets between the two pieces of card on either side. Staple together the pile along one side. Staple from both sides if the staples do not go all the way through.

Hammer the stapled side to avoid any rogue staples sticking out. Cut a strip of card which is the same length as the book and approximately 3–4cm (1¼–1½ in) wide. Glue the strip around the spine with double-sided tape to hide the staples.

Bookmarks

The bookmarks are made from the Tilda decoupage papers and laminated with self-laminating sheets.

Make the tassel by wrapping a bunch of embroidery yarn around your hand. Tie a piece of yarn through the bunch and another around the bunch, before cutting the ends to make tassels.

Presents and Cards

Beautiful cards and gifts are always fun to give away. The notebooks on page 30 make gorgeous gifts and here you can see a few versions using green card.

The motifs on the cards are attached with adhesive foam pads for a 3D effect. The edges on the motifs and the cards have been darkened with a brown ink pad.

PATTERNS

Add seam allowance to all parts of the patterns.

The dashed line marks openings and borders between two different fabrics or where two pattern parts should be sewn together.

'ES' stands for extra seam allowance and marks openings where this is required.

'Double fold' means that the fabric should be folded double at this line.

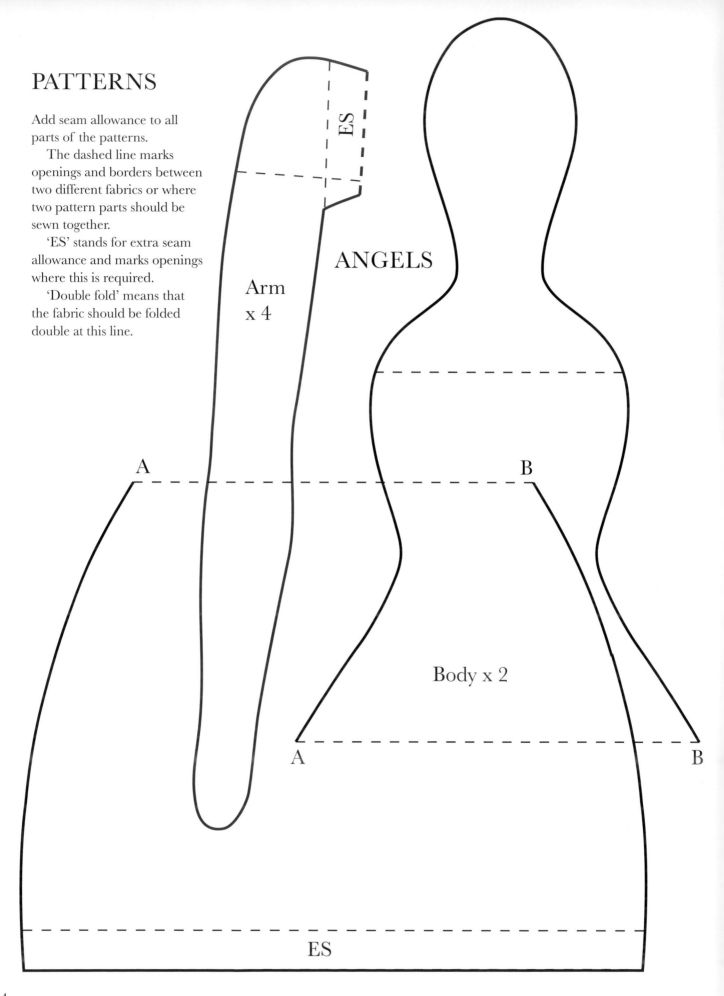

ES

ANGELS

Arm
x 4

A

B

Body x 2

A

B

ES

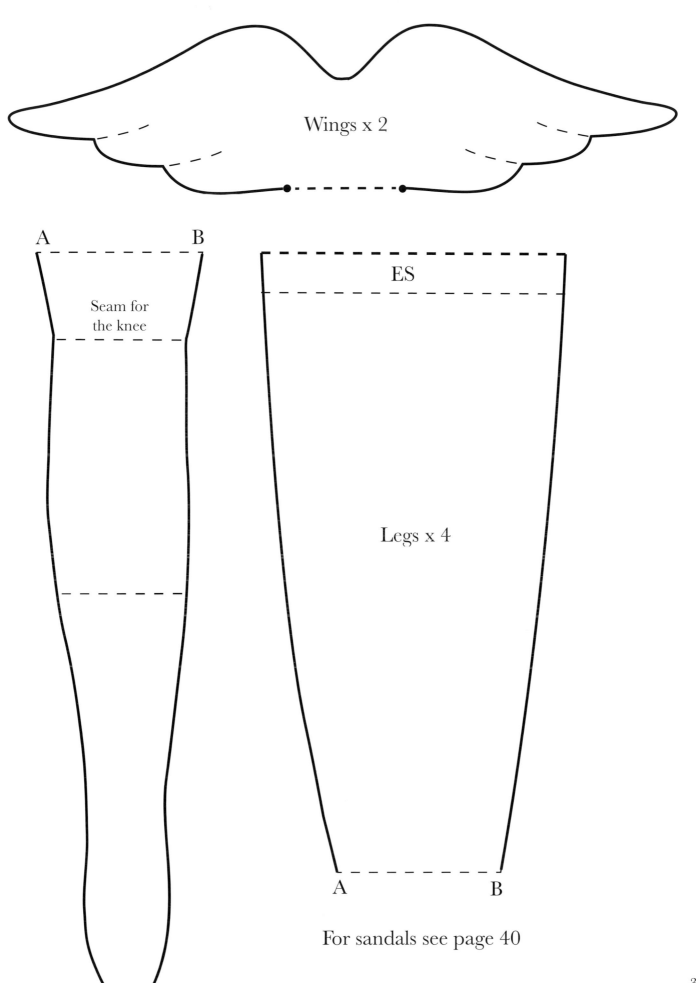

Wings x 2

A   B

Seam for
the knee

ES

Legs x 4

A   B

For sandals see page 40

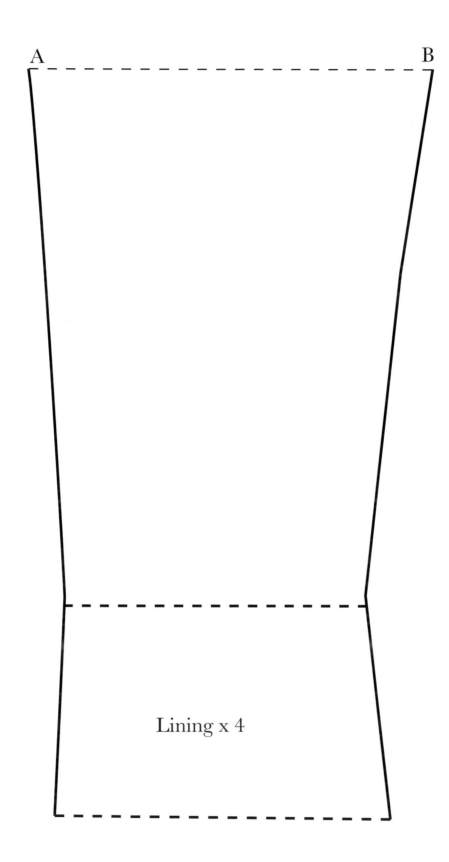

A   B

Lining x 4

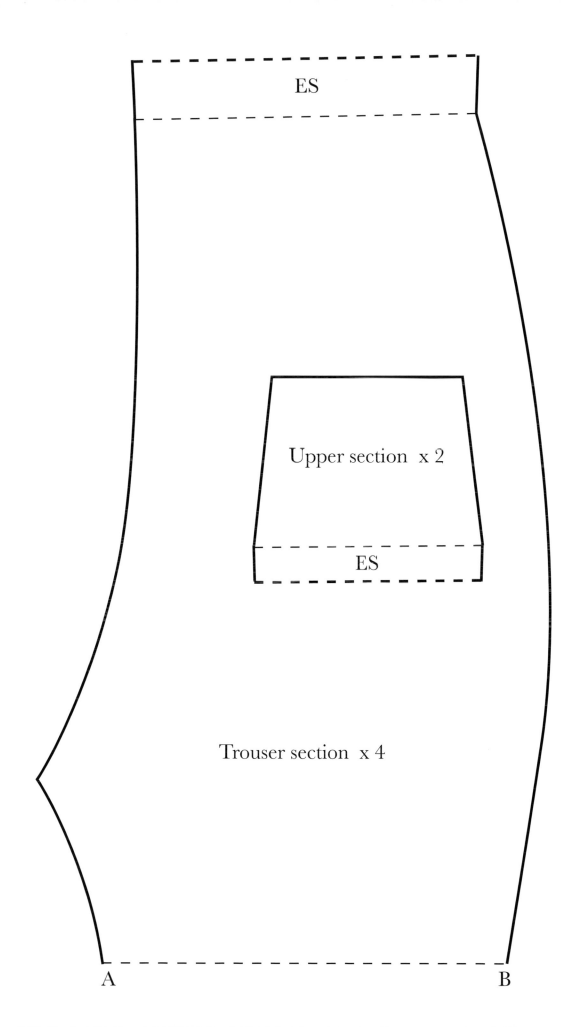

ES

Upper section x 2

ES

Trouser section x 4

A

B

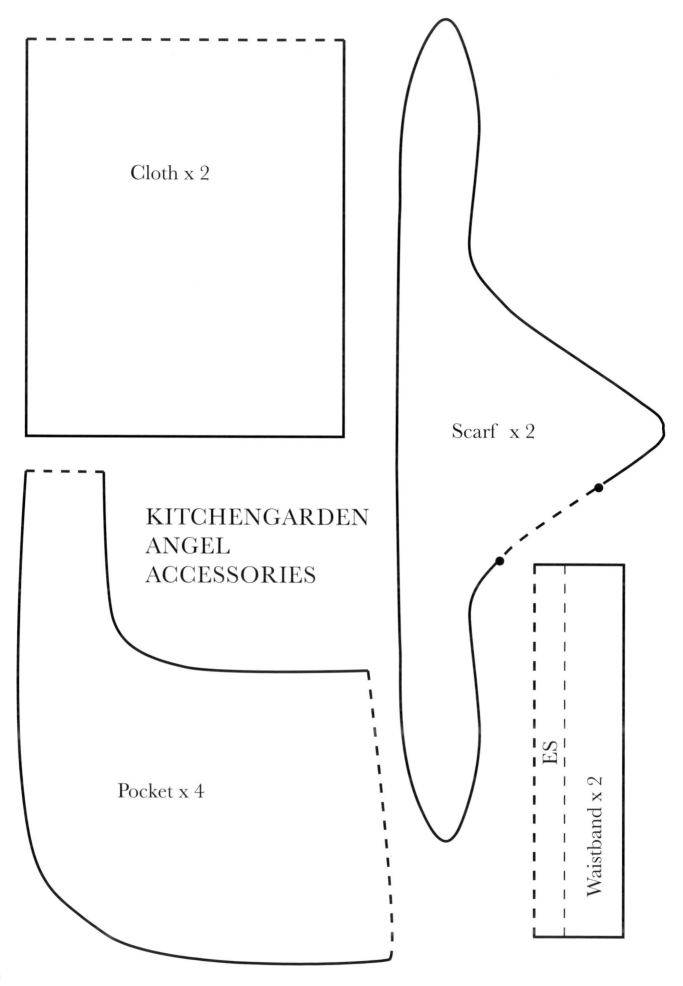

Cloth x 2

Scarf x 2

KITCHENGARDEN
ANGEL
ACCESSORIES

Pocket x 4

ES

Waistband x 2

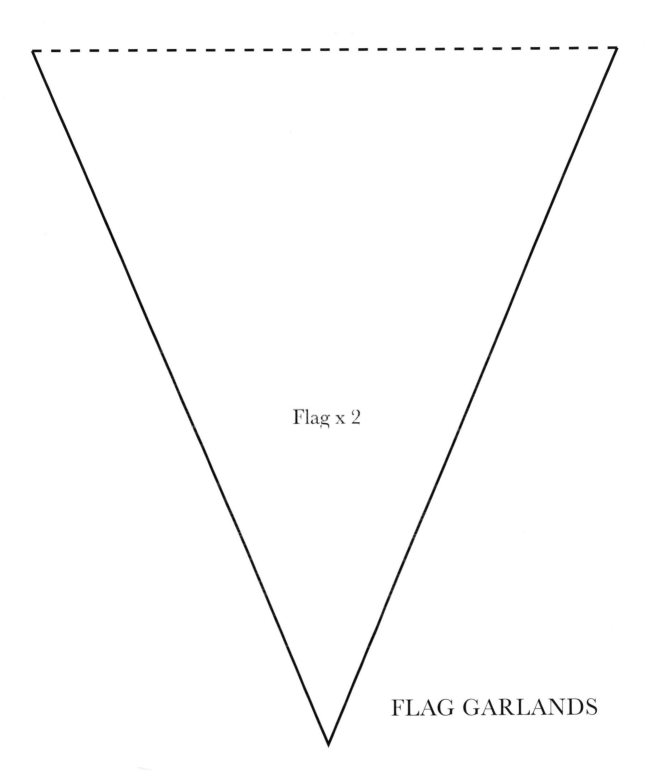

Flag x 2

FLAG GARLANDS

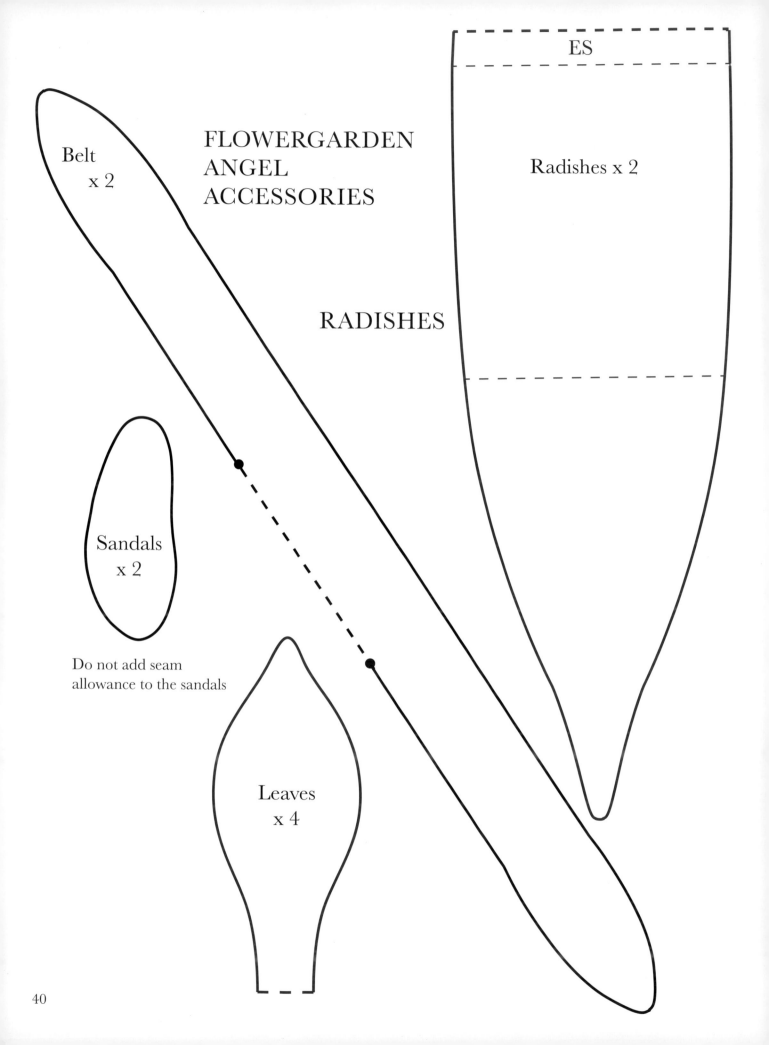

Belt
x 2

FLOWERGARDEN
ANGEL
ACCESSORIES

Radishes x 2

ES

RADISHES

Sandals
x 2

Do not add seam
allowance to the sandals

Leaves
x 4

SUMMER GARLANDS

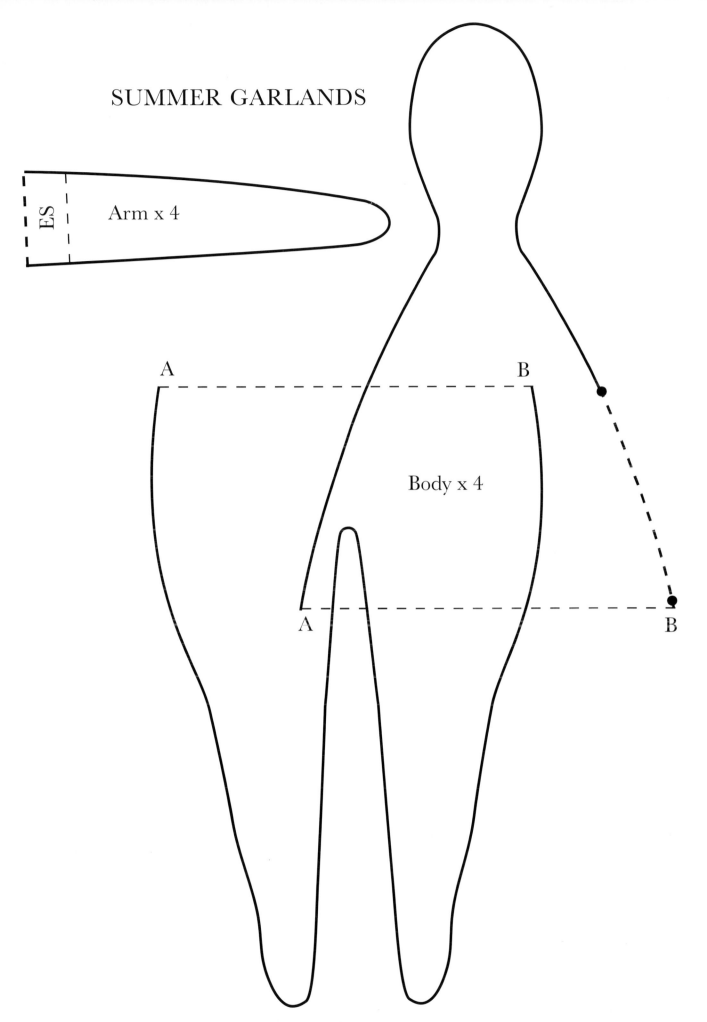

ES

Arm x 4

A   B

Body x 4

A

B

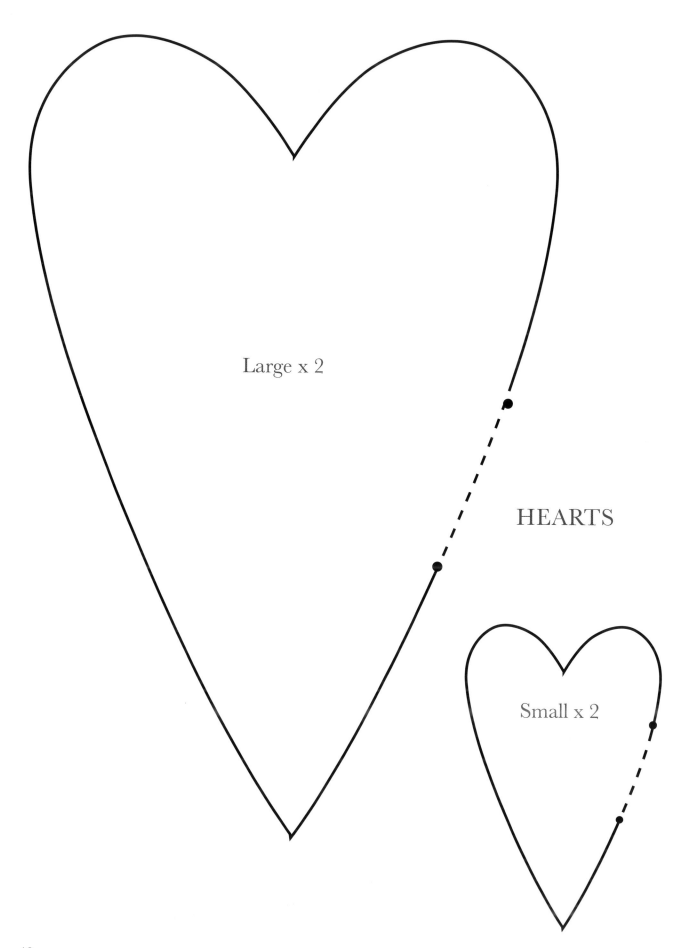

Large x 2

HEARTS

Small x 2

BAG

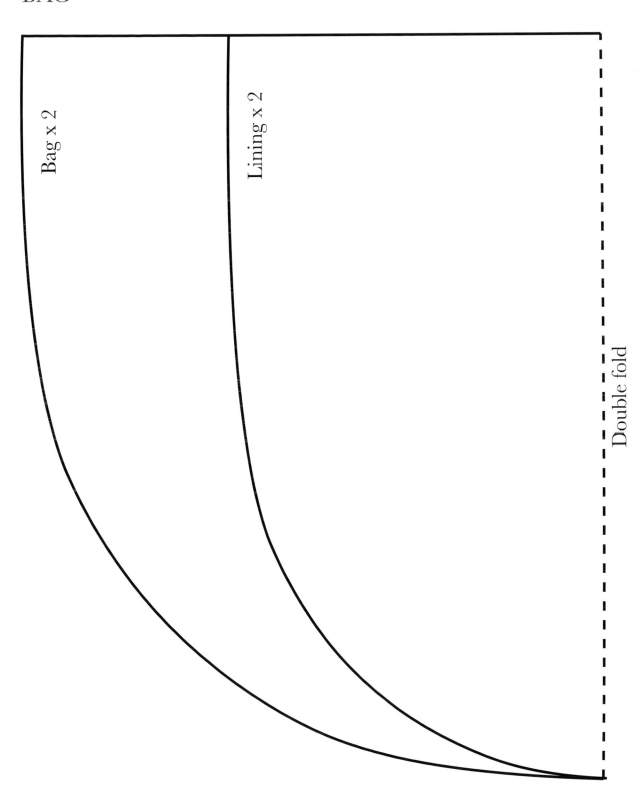

Bag x 2

Lining x 2

Double fold

DALA HORSE

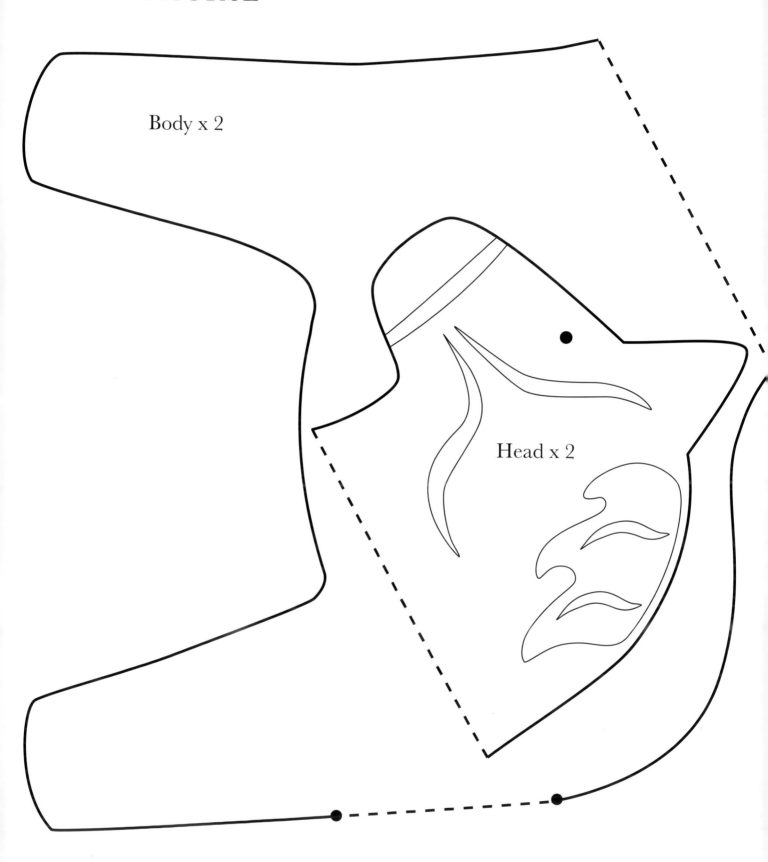

Body x 2

Head x 2

ACCESSORIES

These accessories can be copied using a photocopier, or scanned and printed as decorations for the projects in the book (170–200 gsm matt photo paper is recommended).

GLUE

GLUE

GLUE

GLUE

Seeds

Seeds

GROWN WITH LOVE HOMEGROWN

GROWN WITH LOVE HOMEGROWN

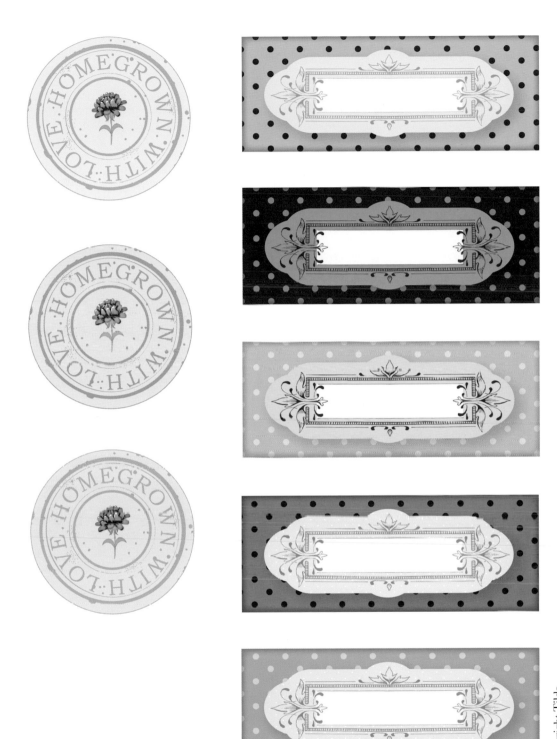

47

Suppliers

UK

Panduro Hobby
Westway House
Transport Avenue
Brentford
Middlesex TW8 9HF
Tel: 020 8566 1680
trade@panduro.co.uk
www.pandurohobby.co.uk

Coast and Country
Crafts & Quilts
8 Sampson Gardens
Ponsanooth
Truro
Cornwall TR3 7RS
Tel: 01872 863894
www.coastandcountry
crafts.co.uk

Fred Aldous Ltd.
37 Lever Street
Manchester M1 1LW
Tel: 08707 517301
www.fredaldous.co.uk

The Fat Quarters
5 Choprell Road
Blackhall Mill
Newcastle NE17 7TN
Tel: 01207 565728
www.thefatquarters.co.uk

The Sewing Bee
52 Hillfoot Street
Dunoon
Argyll PA23 7DT
Tel: 01369 706879
www.thesewingbee.co.uk

Puddlecrafts
7 St. Clair Park
Route Militaire
St. Sampson
Guernsey GY2 4DX
Tel: 01481 245441
www.puddlecrafts.co.uk

Threads and Patches
48 Aylesbury Street
Fenny Stratford
Bletchley
Milton Keynes
MK2 2BU
Tel: 01908 649687
www.threadsand
patches.co.uk

USA

Coats and Clark USA
PO Box 12229
Greenville
SC29612-0229
Tel: 0800 648 1479
www.coatsandclark.com

Connecting Threads
13118 NE 4th Street
Vancouver
WA 9884
www.connecting
threads.com

eQuilter.com
5455 Spine Road,
Suite E
Boulder
CO 80301
www.equilter.com

Hamels Fabrics
5843 Lickman Road
Chilliwack
British Columbia
V2R 4B5
www.hamelsfabrics.com

Keepsake Quilting
Box 1618 Center
Harbor
NH 03226
www.keepsake
quilting.com

The Craft Connection
21055 Front Street
PO Box 1088
Onley
VA 23418
www.craftconn.com

Index